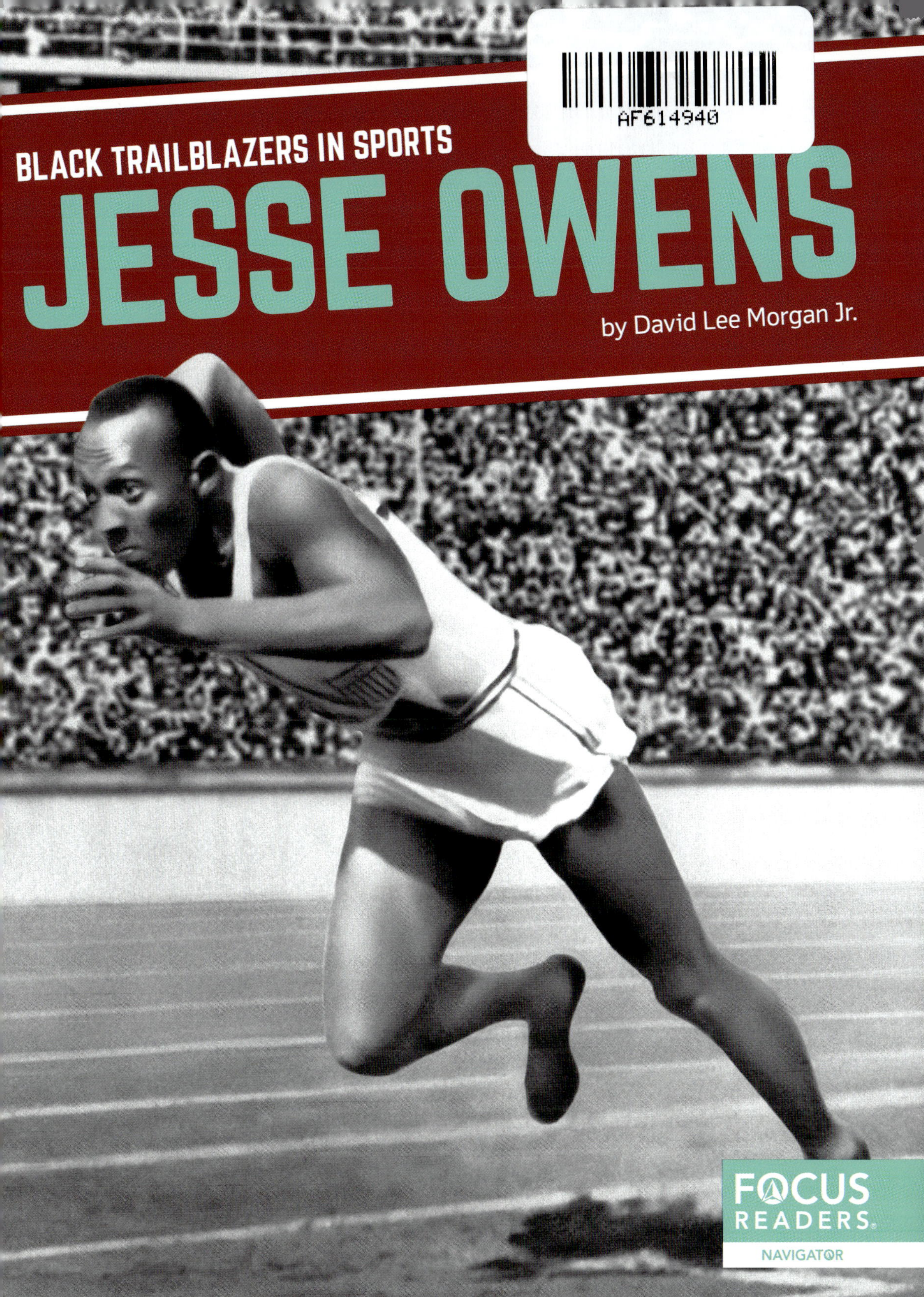
BLACK TRAILBLAZERS IN SPORTS
JESSE OWENS
by David Lee Morgan Jr.
FOCUS READERS
NAVIGATOR

WWW.FOCUSREADERS.COM

Focus Readers is distributed by North Star Editions:
sales@northstareditions.com | 888-417-0195

Produced for Focus Readers by Red Line Editorial.

Photographs ©: Library of Congress, cover, 1; Print Collector/Hulton Archive/Getty Images, 4–5; Bettmann/Getty Images, 7, 13, 15, 16–17, 18, 22–23; picture-alliance/dpa/AP Images, 8; Dorothea Lange/Library of Congress, 10–11; AP Images, 21, 25; Matt Dunham/AP Images, 27; Red Line Editorial, 29

Library of Congress Cataloging-in-Publication Data
Names: Morgan, David Lee, author.
Title: Jesse Owens / by David Lee Morgan, Jr.
Description: Mendota Heights, MN: Focus Readers, [2025] | Series: Black trailblazers in sports | Includes bibliographical references and index. | Audience: Grades 4-6
Identifiers: LCCN 2023054164 (print) | LCCN 2023054165 (ebook) | ISBN 9798889982104 (hardcover) | ISBN 9798889982661 (paperback) | ISBN 9798889983736 (pdf) | ISBN 9798889983224 (ebook)
Subjects: LCSH: Owens, Jesse, 1913-1980--Juvenile literature. | African American track and field athletes--Alabama--Biography--Juvenile literature. | Ohio State University--Sports--History--Juvenile literature. | Olympic athletes--Alabama--Biography--Juvenile literature. | Olympic Games (11th : 1936 : Berlin, Germany)--Juvenile literature. | Olympics--Records. | Racism in sports--Juvenile literature. | Public speaking--Juvenile literature. | Baseball--Coaching--New York. | Medal of Freedom--Juvenile literature.
Classification: LCC GV697.O9 M67 2025 (print) | LCC GV697.O9 (ebook) | DDC 796.42092 [B]--dc23/eng/20231213
LC record available at https://lccn.loc.gov/2023054164
LC ebook record available at https://lccn.loc.gov/2023054165

Printed in the United States of America
Mankato, MN
082024

ABOUT THE AUTHOR

David Lee Morgan Jr. is the author of 11 books, including *LeBron James: The Rise of a Star* and *Breaking Through the Lines: The Marion Motley Story*. Morgan was a longtime sportswriter with the *Akron Beacon Journal* and is now a high school English teacher and public speaker.

TABLE OF CONTENTS

CHAPTER 1

A GOLDEN MOMENT

Jesse Owens stared straight ahead on the track. He was about to run the 100-meter race in the 1936 Olympic Games. A massive crowd watched in Berlin, Germany. Then the starting gun fired. Owens took off. He quickly gained the lead. US teammate Ralph Metcalfe closed in. But Owens was too fast.

Jesse Owens crosses the finish line to win the 100-meter race at the 1936 Olympic Games.

He finished the race in 10.3 seconds. That tied the world record. Owens placed first and won the gold medal.

In 1936, Adolf Hitler was Germany's leader. Hitler held **racist** beliefs. He claimed that some groups of people were not fully human. These groups included Jewish people, Black people, and many others. Hitler expected German athletes to beat Owens at the Olympics. He thought it would prove that German people were better than all others. But Owens showed that Hitler was wrong. And the whole world saw it.

After the 100-meter race, Owens did the long jump. Luz Long was a German

Owens leaps through the air to win gold at the long jump at the 1936 Olympics.

athlete. He competed against Owens in the event. Long didn't care that Owens was Black. Long respected his American competitor. He gave Owens some tips after Owens had a few bad jumps.

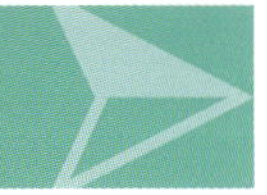
Luz Long and Owens stayed friends for years after the Olympics.

Long's advice helped Owens win the gold medal. Owens set an Olympic record by jumping 26 feet, 5⅜ inches (8.06 m).

Long finished second and won the silver medal. After the event, Long was the first one to congratulate Owens. They later walked around the stadium together in **solidarity**.

Next, Owens won the 200-meter race. He set a world record there. He ran it in 20.7 seconds. Finally, Owens took part in the 4x100-meter relay. Owens and his team won. He became the second American to win four track-and-field gold medals at a single Olympics.

Owens showed millions of people that he was the best runner in the world. He became one of the most famous athletes in Olympic history.

CHAPTER 2

THE RISE OF A TRACK STAR

Jesse Owens was born on September 12, 1913, in Oakville, Alabama. He was the youngest of 10 children. His parents were **sharecroppers**.

When Jesse was five, a large tumor grew on his chest. His parents worried he would stop breathing. But they couldn't afford a doctor. So, Jesse's

Enslaved Black Americans were freed after the US Civil War (1861–1865). But many had to work as sharecroppers and be in debt to white landowners.

mother removed the tumor herself. Jesse survived, and he got better.

Jesse's family moved to Cleveland, Ohio, when he was nine. His path to track began in junior high. The school's gym teacher and track coach saw how athletic Jesse was. He encouraged Jesse to run track.

BECOMING JESSE

Jesse's full name was James Cleveland Owens. When he started school in Ohio, his teacher asked his name. He said it was "J. C." That's what his family called him. But Jesse was from the South. So, he spoke a bit differently than the people in the North. His teacher misheard him and thought he said "Jesse." The name stuck.

Owens was so fast in college that people called him the "Buckeye Bullet."

Jesse joined the team and quickly excelled. He set junior high records in the high jump and long jump. Jesse continued winning in high school. In his senior year, he won three events at a national meet.

When it was time for Owens to go to college, many schools wanted him. Owens decided to attend Ohio State

University. However, the school didn't offer **scholarships** for track and field. As a result, he had to work several jobs.

Because Owens was Black, he wasn't allowed to live in the dorms on campus. Instead, he had to live off campus. And Owens couldn't eat in the same restaurants as his white teammates. Owens often had to order takeout or eat in Black-only restaurants.

But on the track, Owens showed he was one of the best. He became the first Black student to be captain of any Ohio State **varsity** sports team.

Then, on May 25, 1935, Owens made history. That day, he tied the world record

Many people believe Owens's achievement on May 25, 1935, is still the greatest athletic feat of all time.

in the 100-yard dash. Next, he set world records in the long jump, the 220-yard dash, and the 220-yard low hurdles. He did all this in less than an hour.

CHAPTER 3

LOOKING FOR HAPPINESS

Jesse Owens was 22 years old when he won four gold medals at the 1936 Olympic Games. After that, he was ready to return to the United States. Owens wanted to become a professional runner. He thought he would be able to earn good money.

Owens poses with his four gold medals and wears an Olympic wreath after the 1936 Olympics.

Owens waves to fans during his 1936 parade in New York City.

The Amateur Athletic Union (AAU) had other plans. It wanted to take Owens and his teammates all over Europe after the Olympics. The group wanted the athletes to compete in exhibitions. The AAU would make money from these events. However, the athletes wouldn't be paid because they were amateurs.

For this reason, Owens left the team. When he returned to the United States, Owens had a parade in his honor in New York City. But he also experienced racism. For example, there was an event for him at a fancy hotel. But Owens and his family weren't allowed to use the main elevator. They weren't allowed to stay at the hotel, either.

Owens struggled to find a good job. He worked at a gas station for a while. He also earned money in stunt races against dogs and motorcycles. He even raced horses at halftime during sporting events. Owens would start 40 yards (37 m) ahead of the horse. They would race 100 yards (91 m). Owens often won.

Owens did not enjoy these jobs. He felt they were **degrading**. But he had to make

WORLD WAR II

World War II took place between 1939 and 1945. As a result, there were no Olympic Games in 1940 or 1944. But Owens was able to find jobs. In 1942, he worked for the US government. He led a national fitness program for Black Americans. The next year, Owens went to the Ford Motor Company in Detroit, Michigan. He helped hire Black workers for the company.

Owens races against a horse in 1948.

money to support his wife and children. One thing Owens enjoyed was working with kids. He found a job working as a playground director in Cleveland. This type of work made him happy.

LAUNDERED TO PERFECTION
individually CELLOPHANE WRAPPED
GOLD SEAL LAUNDRY DIVISION OF....
LEADER CLEANERS
FOLLOW THE Leader FOR BETTER CLEANING

CHAPTER 4

LEAVING HIS LEGACY

In 1949, Jesse Owens and his family moved to Chicago, Illinois. There, Owens started a career as a public speaker. He talked about **sportsmanship** and love. He spoke about happiness and being kind to one another, regardless of skin color. He started to earn a steady income.

Owens sought many business opportunities throughout his life. For example, in the 1950s, he co-owned a cleaning service in Chicago.

This work led to other opportunities. In 1955, President Dwight D. Eisenhower named Owens US **Ambassador** of Sports. Owens traveled all over the world. He supported amateur sports programs. The next year, Owens attended the 1956 Summer Olympic Games in Melbourne, Australia. He was one of Eisenhower's personal representatives.

Owens even worked in Major League Baseball. He became the spring training baserunning coach for the New York Mets in 1965. Owens also stayed connected with the Olympic Games. He joined the US Olympic Committee in 1973. He helped raise money to train US athletes.

President Gerald Ford pins the Presidential Medal of Freedom on Owens at the White House in 1976.

In 1974, Owens entered the National Track and Field Hall of Fame. In 1976, President Gerald Ford presented Owens with the Presidential Medal of Freedom. It is the highest non-military honor of the US government. He received this great honor 40 years after winning his gold medals in Berlin.

On March 31, 1980, Owens died of lung cancer. He was 66 years old. Owens left a proud **legacy**. For example, in 2001, Ohio State University built a new stadium. The college named it the Jesse Owens Memorial Stadium. A statue of Owens

JESSE-OWENS-ALLEE

In 1984, Berlin honored Owens. The city renamed one of its streets "Jesse-Owens-Allee." ***Allee*** **means "avenue" in German. This street is near the stadium where the 1936 Olympics took place. Owens won his four gold medals in that stadium. Owens's family attended the renaming ceremony as guests of the German government.**

People use Jesse-Owens-Allee every day in Berlin, keeping his legacy alive.

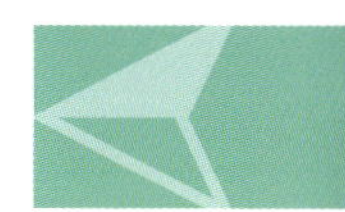

stands outside the building. It shows four gold medals hanging around his neck.

Owens was one of the best track stars of the 1900s. People remember him as a great athlete, husband, and father. He fought racism in Germany and in the United States. He loved teaching sportsmanship to young people.

JESSE OWENS

- **Height:** 5 feet 10 inches (178 cm)
- **Weight:** 165 pounds (75 kg)
- **Born:** September 12, 1913
- **Died:** March 31, 1980
- **Birthplace:** Oakville, Alabama
- **High school:** East Technical High School (Cleveland, OH)
- **College:** Ohio State University (Columbus, OH) (1933–36, 1940–41)
- **Major achievements:** 100-meter Olympic gold medal (1936); 200-meter Olympic gold medal (1936); long jump Olympic gold medal (1936); 400-meter relay Olympic gold medal (1936); Associated Press Athlete of the Year (1936); National Track and Field Hall of Fame (1974); Presidential Medal of Freedom (1976); US Olympic Hall of Fame (1983)

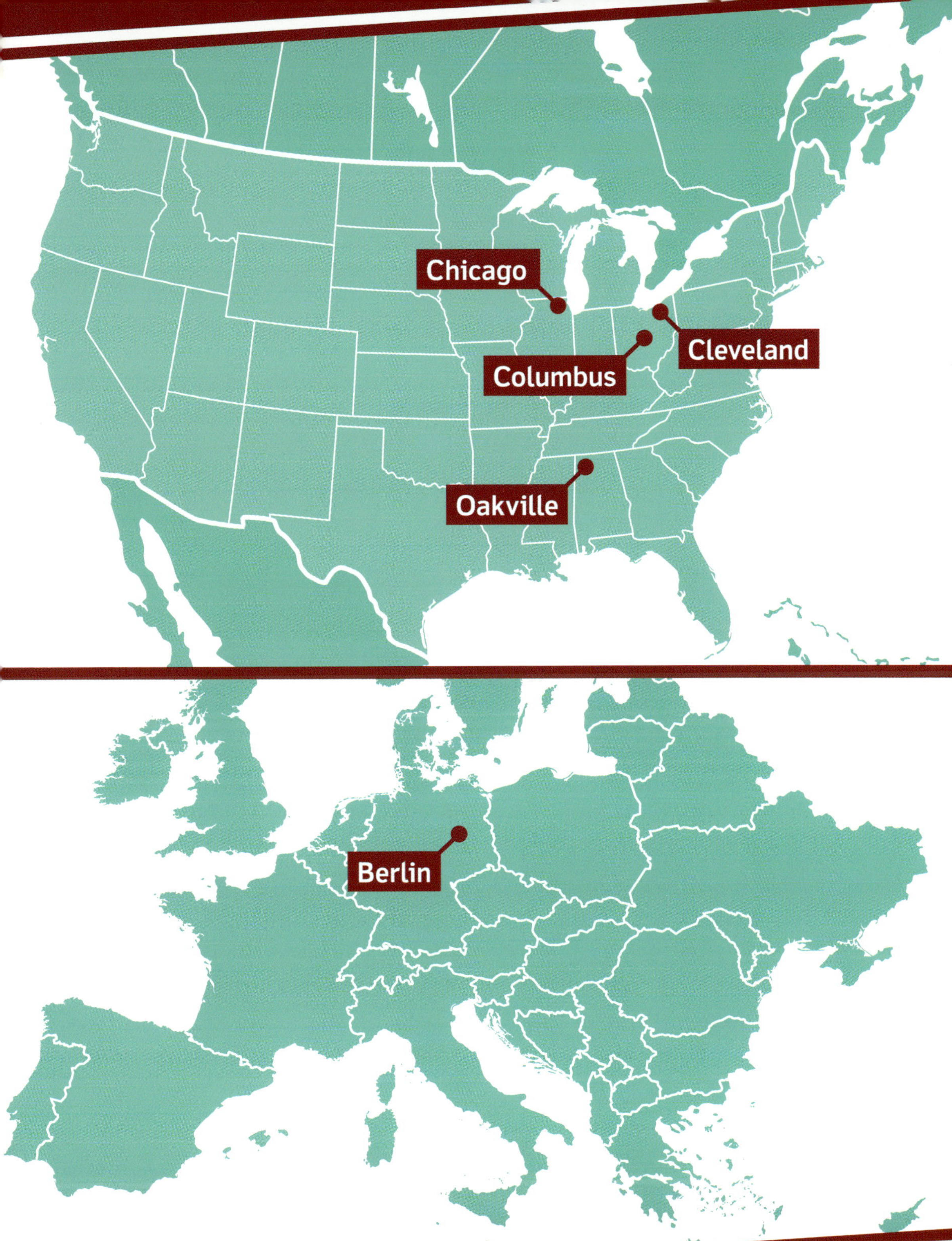
Chicago
Cleveland
Columbus
Oakville
Berlin

FOCUS ON
JESSE OWENS

Write your answers on a separate sheet of paper.

1. Write a paragraph explaining the main ideas of Chapter 2.
2. Do you think Jesse Owens's 1935 record-breaking performance or 1936 Olympic Games performance is more impressive? Why?
3. Where did the 1936 Olympic Games take place?
   A. Australia
   B. Germany
   C. the United States
4. In 1949, what job did Owens get that helped him make good money?
   A. racing against horses
   B. working at a gas station
   C. public speaking

Answer key on page 32.

GLOSSARY

ambassador
An official representative of a country.

degrading
Putting someone down or making them feel bad about themselves.

legacy
The things a person becomes known for.

racist
Having to do with hatred or mistreatment of people because of their skin color or ethnicity.

scholarships
Money given to students to pay for education expenses.

sharecroppers
Farmers who rent land from its owner and give some of their crops in exchange for working the land.

solidarity
Supporting a person or group and the values they hold.

sportsmanship
Competing in a fair and respectful way.

varsity
The top team representing a high school or college in a sport or competition.

TO LEARN MORE

BOOKS

Buckley, James Jr. *Jesse Owens*. New York: DK Publishing, 2020.

Hoena, Blake. *Jesse Owens: Athletes Who Made a Difference*. Minneapolis: Lerner Publications, 2020.

Walker, Tracy Sue. *Jesse Owens: Track-and-Field Legend*. Minneapolis: Lerner Publications, 2023.

NOTE TO EDUCATORS

Visit **www.focusreaders.com** to find lesson plans, activities, links, and other resources related to this title.

INDEX

Answer Key: 1. Answers will vary; **2.** Answers will vary; **3.** B; **4.** C